To Joy,

It's a pleasure to know you and have you as a colleague.

Blessings to you and your family. Cherish the love!

Nancy

4/28/06

# She's My Grandmother...

*Nancy Massa*

Bloomington, IN  authorHOUSE™ Milton Keynes, UK

*AuthorHouse*™
*1663 Liberty Drive, Suite 200*
*Bloomington, IN 47403*
*www.authorhouse.com*
*Phone: 1-800-839-8640*

*AuthorHouse*™ *UK Ltd.*
*500 Avebury Boulevard*
*Central Milton Keynes, MK9 2BE*
*www.authorhouse.co.uk*
*Phone: 08001974150*

*First published by AuthorHouse* 3/23/2006

*ISBN: 1-4259-1552-3 (sc)*

Library of Congress Control Number: 2006900577

*Printed in the United States of America*
*Bloomington, Indiana*

*This book is printed on acid-free paper.*

# *Chapter 1*

————— ⋙ ‹ ⋘ —————

"I'm going down to see Mom-Mom!" Joey called after he got down from his high chair at the kitchen table. Now that he was three, he didn't use the tray on his high chair, but the height of the chair was just perfect to push up to the kitchen table for his meals.

His trip down the stairs was always the same, his left hand was on the railing, his left foot went on the step down and then the right foot came down to meet the left. His pace was as rapid as he could make it because Joey was anticipating his happy visit with Mom-Mom, in her cozy apartment downstairs.

"OK, Hon, have fun," his Mom called after him.

"Woo-hoo," he called out while knocking and opening the door to Mom-Mom's apartment. "Woo-hoo," her voice called out in return, and into Mom-Mom's Joey went, closing the door behind him.

He was very good about remembering to close her door because he knew that his dog, Nipsy, was not allowed in Mom-Mom's, not because she didn't love him but because he shed his hair and sometimes he had fleas!

His entry was through her bedroom, which had a bed with a flowered spread on his right (a bed he had helped Mom-Mom make many times, carefully lifting up the bed spread on one side of the bed as she instructed and assisted from the other side). There was a big mahogany vanity along the wall in front of him, which had seven drawers. Each drawer held some of

Mom-Mom's treasures. There were two very large mirrors hung on two walls (one behind the vanity and the other on the wall to his left). His head was barely high enough for him to see himself in them.

He took a left through the door opening and there he was, in Mom-Mom's kitchen and living room. "Hi Mom-Mom," he said giving her a hug around her waist. "Hello, sweetheart, how was your day?" she asked as she dried her dinner dishes and put them away. Joey told her of his busy day in preschool, about his friends there and his adventures at the babysitter's after that. Both his Mom and Dad worked so he went to preschool and the babysitter on weekdays.

"What shall we do tonight?" asked Mom-Mom, with the sounds of Jeopardy coming from her TV in the background. "Do you want to bowl or shall we read a book?" "Bowl!" Joey quickly answered. "Well you'd better get the pins then," she said with a smile. He went back into her bedroom, to the big vanity, opened the middle drawer on the left and took out a zippered bag of Mom-Mom's pink, plastic hair curlers and the tennis ball that was patiently waiting for the next bowling game. "OK, set them up," she said and together they set ten pink, plastic hair curlers up on end and 'bowled' them over with the tennis ball over and over again. This was one of Joey's favorite Mom-Mom inventions and he requested it quite often.

"I think it's about time for you to go to bed, you have a busy day tomorrow. Let's put the 'pins' away." They both put the curlers in the zippered bag and after Joey put it back in the middle drawer on the left of the vanity, he and Mom-Mom looked at their reflection in the big mirror. "Now, let's see how tall you're getting. Wow, all the way up to here!" She had taken her hand and drawn an imaginary line from the top of his head to the corresponding spot on her. Tonight he was as tall as her waist. This was another favorite Mom-Mom invention for Joey. He loved to see how big he was getting. Joey and Mom-Mom said goodnight and he went back up the stairs the same way he had come down, left foot up, right foot to meet it.

# *Chapter 2*

━━━◆◆◆━━━

Joey's Mom and Dad had bought their house about a year earlier. It was called a bilevel and their living room, kitchen, dining room and bedrooms were upstairs. It had an apartment right in it, downstairs, next to the den and spare bedroom. They wanted Mom-Mom to live with them. She was seventy-six years old and they didn't want her to be living by herself in case she got sick or needed help. This was perfect. She had her own home in their home, played golf, visited with her family and friends, took vacations, did her laundry, prepared her own meals, planted her flower garden and got to see her sweetheart, Joey, every day. She always had special treats for him. Sometimes they would sit cuddled on the couch and she would read to him. Sometimes, as they sat on the couch together they would play the hand-pat game. Mom-Mom would slowly slide her hand along the cushion and Joey would try to quickly pat it, while Mom-

Mom moved her hand quickly away. There was always a cookie for Joey in the cookie tin that was on top of the refrigerator. When they were feeling very fancy, Mom-Mom would pour apple juice into her cut glass goblets and they would pretend to be drinking some 'apple wine'.

Some visits were in the yard because Joey enjoyed outside activities a lot and Mom-Mom did too. Sometimes he would be practicing T-ball and she would be cheering him on. Other times she would be hanging up her laundry on the clothesline and he and she would have a quiet conversation. Other times they would throw the stick for Nipsy to fetch. In the fall, Mom-Mom helped rake the leaves in the yard, designing a huge pile so that Joey could jump in it.

On Halloween, Joey the pirate (or clown or Ninja) was in his costume, ready for his candy gathering through the neighborhood. He left his house through the front door, went to the side door, which was Mom-Mom's, knocked and said his first "Trick or Treat!" of the day. She opened her door and always acted surprised and impressed with his costume. "Here you are, Mr. Pirate," as she gave him his treat, "Happy Halloween."

Thanksgiving was a holiday that sometimes had two celebrations because Mom-Mom's birthday was in November and every once in a while Thanksgiving and her birthday were on the same day. Joey's aunts and uncles and cousins would come to his house for Thanksgiving and it was so much fun. One year Joey sang "You Are My Sunshine" to Mom-Mom for her birthday and she was so happy that she had tears of happiness in her eyes and she gave him an extra tight hug for making her feel so special.

No presents could be opened on Christmas morning until Mom-Mom joined the family, which was never later than 7:30 in the morning. They gathered in the living room by the Christmas tree and, one by one, opened their gifts, with Nipsy helping because he was very good at taking off wrapping paper and not damaging the gift. They would eat breakfast, rest for a while and then go to Joey's other grandmother's house for a big Christmas dinner with his aunts, uncles, cousins and more presents.

Joey was born on Easter Sunday. His birthday did not often fall on the same day as Easter but a birthday celebration was included when his family came over for a great Easter egg hunt and dinner.

Mom-Mom shared in all of these celebrations and all of the family fun.

Summer time was spent swimming at friends' neighborhood pools and at the beach, bike riding, playing with friends, playing with cousins, learning tennis and golf and baseball and soccer. Of all of these activities Mom-Mom liked golf, and she played in the spring, summer and fall. When Joey was five and his family felt that backyard golf and driving range visits had prepared him well enough, he, Mom and Dad and Mom-Mom went to play at a real par-3 golf course. He didn't hit the ball too far but he learned golf, golf

manners and received encouragement

from them all.

# *Chapter 3*

———————◇———————

As 'big kids' school (public school) started for Joey, so did more fun and new activities. He was a busy boy who bubbled with enthusiasm for everything he did.

Visits with Mom-Mom always continued but with all of his other activities, the visits became fewer. He noticed that Mom-Mom was forgetting that she had already said something and would tell him the same story over and over again. She started to call him her son's name, instead of "Joey." He would remind her, "I'm Joey, Mom-Mom." She would say "Oh that's right," and she would forget again. After a while, he didn't remind her what his name was thinking it might embarrass her because she didn't remember.

Holiday celebrations started to be too confusing and too crowded feeling for Mom-Mom. She was invited to go to Joey's aunt's house for

Thanksgiving dinner the week before Thanksgiving and she got so confused that she got dressed up every day that week, thinking it was Thanksgiving. "Today isn't Thanksgiving, Mom-Mom. That's Thursday, today is only Monday (Tuesday, Wednesday). By the time Thanksgiving did come, Mom-Mom was confused and upset and didn't want to come to dinner.

Christmas dinner at Nanny's was too loud and confusing for Mom-Mom, so Joey's Mom arranged for her to spend a quiet Christmas with her niece.

The excitement and noise that

naturally comes about when children play started to bother Mom-Mom. Just going up and down the steps created quite an uproar since Joey now took the one-foot-on-a-step approach at lightning speed. The stairs in his house got a lot of traffic on them because they were the only path to the front door and, through the den downstairs, to the back door. As Joey and his friends were on the way downstairs to go outside, Mom-Mom opened her door at the bottom of the steps and confronted them with an upset tone, "What is the ruckus? It sounds like a herd of elephants crashing through my ceiling!" "Nothing, Mom-Mom, we're just going outside," Joey replied. "Well you're too noisy; I'm losing my mind. I am not going to stay in this place any more. I'm going to leave and take my things with me. What are you building, with all that banging?" Joey and his friends had nervous giggles in response. They had no idea how to answer Mom-Mom. Joey's Mom had to try to explain that no one was building anything. It was just the sound of the kids on the stairs. Joey and his friends tried very hard to play quietly in the house and save the loudness for outside.

Mom-Mom began to put her wallet in a 'safe place' because she was worried that someone would take it, and then she forgot where she put it. She again scolded him for taking her wallet, "You're not to touch my things." "I didn't take your wallet, Mom-Mom, but I'll help you look for it. Is it the red one?" Joey would then look under cushions, under furniture in the living room and in cabinets in the kitchen until he found the red wallet that she had misplaced. In fact, everyone in the house took turns looking for the red wallet because Mom-Mom started to misplace it every day.

Mom-Mom couldn't drive anymore because it wasn't safe. That meant that Joey's Mom did her shopping, made her meals, did her laundry, and took her to church, the doctor's or wherever she had to go. This became very hard to do because she worked as a speech therapist in the local school system and was busy with that job and Joey and his Dad. So she hired a companion to come in the afternoons to keep Mom-Mom company and to fix her dinners. Joey would go visiting with Mom-Mom and the companions. There were a few different people hired for this job because Mom-Mom did not like some of the people hired and became very upset about having them come. Sometimes she locked her door, sometimes she sent them away from the door and sometimes she sent them away once they had been there for a while. Mom-Mom became very lonely and unhappy. During the day she was alone while Joey and his Mom went to school and his Dad went to work. She sometimes stayed in her bathrobe all day and waited until Joey and his Mom got home from school. Almost every day there was something planned after school (soccer practice, art lessons, cub scouts, basketball, and baseball) and Mom-Mom would feel left out, but she didn't want to go to the activity with them.

# Chapter 4

So Joey's Mom found an adult activity center for Mom-Mom that would pick her up in the morning and bring her home in the afternoon. There were people her age there and they had a very nice lunch and many activities. They went to visit the center to see if Mom-Mom would like it and Joey went too. He could always make

Mom-Mom feel relaxed and comfortable. It was a big house down by the beach and it had big doors, high ceilings and big rooms. There were crafts, nice people teaching and directing activities, areas to sit and relax, an area to sit and eat, and a room for physical fitness. The people who went to the center were all older people, some would talk and not make too much sense, but they all seemed very nice. When Mom-Mom arrived, they were just starting a physical fitness activity and they wanted her to join in. She didn't want to but Joey went with her, encouraging her to come and participate. Joey's Mom stayed with the director and filled out the paperwork to have Mom-Mom go to the activity center. When she was finished and went to find them to leave, she found the folks seated in a big circle throwing and catching a big beach ball to some lively music. Part of the circle was Joey and Mom-Mom, taking their turns catching and throwing and grooving to the music. It made Joey's Mom smile when she saw them, to see how special they were to each other and how much they loved each other, and to see that Mom-Mom was having fun. As they left, Joey's Mom asked Mom-Mom how she liked the center and Mom-

Mom said she didn't like it. "They all have problems," she said, "I can't be expected to solve all those people's problems." The smile of hope left Joey's Mom and they drove home.

The activity center and the companion in the afternoon were successful for a while, but that was not the case for very long. Mom-Mom did not want to go to the center, and the van came early in the morning while Joey and his Mom were getting ready for school and his Dad was getting ready for work. They could not help Mom-Mom get ready for the van in the morning so it became necessary to hire another caregiver to come at six

o'clock in the morning to get Mom-Mom

ready and encourage her to go.

# Chapter 5

By this time Joey was in second grade and his parents had explained to him that Mom-Mom was behaving the way she was because of a disease called Alzheimer's. He had long ago noticed the change in Mom-Mom but did not know the cause or the name. This past birthday, she had not known that it was his birthday (his Mom had bought an extra present for him and pretended it was from Mom-Mom). There were no extra Halloween treats for him, Thanksgiving was a Thanksgiving celebration without Mom-Mom's birthday because she went to her niece's home for a quiet dinner, and that Christmas morning Joey and his family waited until almost nine o'clock in the morning and Mom-Mom had not come upstairs yet. Joey had to go and wake her up, wondering, "How could anyone forget Christmas?" She sat with the family and opened her presents, but she did not know what this special day was anymore.

Then, during that winter, at four o'clock in the morning, there was a loud banging on the front door, which woke up everyone in the house. The loud banging continued until Joey's Mom and Dad rushed to the front door and opened it. A policeman was standing there and another policeman was standing at the bottom of the steps with Mom-Mom, in her nightclothes with a blanket around her shoulders that they had given her, looking very cold and confused. She had gone outside in the middle of the night, dressed only in her nightclothes, and wandered down the street. The policemen happened to be driving down the road, saw her and brought her back home. This was very upsetting for Joey's Mom and Dad because they understood that it wasn't safe for Mom-Mom in their home anymore. She was going to have to live somewhere where care could be given all day and all night.

# Chapter 6

━━━━━━━━━━━━━━━━━━━

Joey's Mom visited nursing homes for weeks, to find one that would be good for Mom-Mom. The people who live in a nursing home can not take care of themselves anymore and walking into one can be a little scary. A lot of the people in the nursing homes were like Mom-Mom, older and with Alzheimer's disease. They talked about things that were confusing, or didn't talk and sat, staring silently. The hardest thing to see were the people who sat in the hall in special chairs, who couldn't talk anymore, but made sounds and moans. This was not a situation that Joey's Mom and Dad wanted for Mom-Mom; it was the last choice, but it had to be made because they could no longer take care of her in their house. This was the safest place for her.

Mom-Mom had to be told that she was going on vacation as her suitcase was being packed with her clothes and some special belongings that the nursing home recommended bringing. Otherwise, she would not have gone. The whole family brought her to the nursing home. They were very nice there. They gave Mom-Mom a bracelet that wouldn't come off, that set off an alarm if she walked too close to the Exit doors, and they gave her a room right across from the nurse's station, in case she needed help or got lonely. Her roommate was very nice but she couldn't walk anymore so she was in her bed a lot. They had a big dining room in the nursing home, and a big glass room called a solarium, which had a TV, a piano, couches, chairs, and daily activities for everyone who lived there. There was a beauty shop so Mom-Mom could get her hair done and there was a pretty patio outside where you could sit and enjoy the fresh air. This was Mom-Mom's new home and Joey and his family were going to try their best to make her happy.

It was a twenty minute drive to the nursing home, so visits were not as easy as walking down the stairs. Joey went with his Mom a few times a week to visit Mom-Mom. Each time was an experience that was new to everyone. Going into the nursing home was pretty and pleasant. There was a garden with a flowing brook by the entrance. The lobby was neatly decorated with couches and armchairs. The hallway from the lobby to Mom-Mom's room was more like a hospital. It had tile floors and rooms on either side. The hall-sitting people (those people who were not aware of their surroundings) were markers that you had to walk past to get to Mom-Mom's room. Sometimes they would be talking and you couldn't understand what they were saying, sometimes they moaned, and sometimes they sat quietly. It felt like it was a long walk to get to Mom-Mom's room. Joey understood that there was a cause for the condition of these people, but it was not a comfortable feeling when he and his Mom walked down the hall.

Things were better once the visits with Mom-Mom began. Sometimes they would walk to the dining room or the outside patio or the solarium. When Mom-Mom saw Joey's and her reflection in a window in the solarium, she performed her measurement routine, "Look how tall you're getting! You're almost as tall as I am," as she drew the imaginary line from his head to her body it came to her eyebrows. When she did this, it amazed Joey's Mom that Mom-Mom still had this routine in her memory bank. Sometimes they would just stay in Mom-Mom's room and watch TV and visit. In the fall, when the leaves were beautiful colors, Joey and his Mom and Dad would take Mom-Mom for rides in the car to see the beautiful scenery. She liked that a lot. It was a little tricky to leave the nursing home and enter back in on these trips because Mom-Mom's bracelet always set off the loud alarm, and the nurse had to come to the Exit door, make sure everything was all right and turn the alarm off.

# *Chapter 7*

—————————•◊•◊•—————————

One day, as Mom-Mom, Joey and his Mom were walking down the hall back to Mom-Mom's room, they noticed a crowd of people and loud talking at the nurse's station, which was across the hall from Mom-Mom's room. The nurse's station was a popular gathering spot after meals, so the number of people was not unusual, but the voices were definitely loud and sounding upset and this caused a cautious feeling as they approached. Mom-Mom escorted Joey to the right of the hall, closest to the nurse's station, through the standing people, the seated people, and the people in wheelchairs. They scooted into her room and closed the door behind them. As they were on their way to the room, the problem in the hall unfolded.

One of the residents, who was in a wheelchair, became very upset about something and had ripped a notice off of the bulletin board, as well as the pushpins that had held it up on the board. She was very angry and was crumpling the paper and angrily talking. Some of the people in the hall were trying to talk to her about whatever the problem was, but this just made her more agitated. She took a pushpin in her hand and stuck it in the leg of one of the ladies. "Ouch, she stabbed me in the leg," the lady shouted. "Watch out, she's got a tack. She's crazy!" she said to Joey's Mom, who had gotten mingled in with the crowd because she was on the left side of the hall and was trying to get around the lady in the wheelchair with the tack. Just as she had walked around the lady in the wheelchair, whose back was to her, the lady swung the wheelchair around with her feet, facing Joey's Mom. She held the pushpin up in the air and in a furious voice said to Joey's Mom, "You think this is funny? I'll show you, I'm going to shove this right up your *??" as she made quick, stabbing motions at Joey's Mom with the pushpin. A nurse came and wheeled the lady away and Joey's Mom quickly opened the door to Mom-Mom's room and escaped the confusion in the hall, closing the door behind her. She felt a little weak from what just had happened and wanted to sit down for a moment. As she turned from the door and faced the room, she saw Joey, seated cross-legged on Mom-Mom's bed and Mom-Mom, seated facing him in her lounge chair calmly playing the hand-pat game on the surface of the bed. Joey's Mom told them of her peril in the hall and Joey responded without even lifting his gaze up from the bed surface, "Mom-Mom got me right into her room. She said she hates when they do that." Then he went right back to the hand-pat game and instead of moving his hand away, he allowed Mom-Mom to capture his hand and hold it for a few moments.

Joey's Mom's mind was racing as she sat and composed herself after the tack incident. She was concerned that this kind of behavior would be a little too scary for Joey to experience. She thought that perhaps he wouldn't want to visit Mom-Mom as much, and that would be all right with her; he was only nine years old, after all.

They stayed a little while longer

that day and then it was time to go. The hall was quiet again with just the regular 'sitting in the hall people'. Mom-Mom walked down the hall too and thought she was leaving with Joey and his Mom and her bracelet set off the loud alarm at the Exit door again. The nurse came and took Mom-Mom back into the lobby and Joey and his Mom continued walking silently toward the car.

"You know, Hon, you don't have to come to visit Mom-Mom as much if it upsets you. This was a pretty crazy day today," Joey's Mom said. Joey stopped, turned to his Mom and said to her in a kind, calm, very grown-up way, "She's my Grandmother, and I would do anything for her."

Her heart was flooded with love for Joey and for Mom-Mom and her eyes filled with silent tears as she got in the car. Joey had reminded her how pure love felt, that open, giving, intense, joyful true love that children are able to feel. He loved Mom-Mom so deeply that her behavior now or her living arrangements couldn't change or take that love away. Joey's Mom felt that beautiful pure love for Joey, because he was her son, and again, for Mom-Mom because she was her mother.

Joey's Mom patted his knee and told him she loved him, as she drove out of the parking lot and headed home.

## *About the Author*

Nancy M. Massa, a lifelong resident of New Jersey resides in Eatontown with her husband and her son, who is now in college. She has a BA in Speech from Douglass College and an MA in Human Development from Fairleigh Dickinson University. She has been a speech correctionist in the Eatontown Public School District for 33 years and has enjoyed working with and learning from children of various ages and abilities, in grades Kindergarten through Middle School.

The story she has written, *She's My Grandmother...*, was inspired by a segment of her family's life. Her mother lived with her family in her elder years and became afflicted with Alzheimer's Disease. Her son's personification of love and life during this difficult period of their family's life, gave her a reawakened perspective and appreciation of how a child experiences life and love and adversity. She has realized and tries to show in this book that even the darkest moments in life have a blessing, if one could look at the situation in a different perspective, perhaps through the eyes of and with the feelings of a child.

She hopes that all readers of this book are able to experience warm hearts, fond memories of their own childhood and grandparents, catch a glimpse of a child's perspective, and be reminded of the pure, unconditional love that a child experiences and is able to give.

Printed in the United States
47879LVS00001B/436-483